WH HAPPENED?

AND OTHER QUESTIONS EVERYONE IS ASKING ABOUT THE CREDIT CRUNCH

Hugh Pym & Nick Kochan

Old St PUBLISHING

First published in 2008 by Old Street Publishing Ltd
28-32 Bowling Green Lane, London EC1R 0BJ
www.oldstreetpublishing.co.uk

ISBN 978 1 905847 92 1

Typeset by Old Street Publishing.
Printed and bound in Great Britain by Clays Ltd, St Ives plc.

Contents

Section 3: How will the crisis affect me?

Introduction

In this fast-moving story, any account is bound to be imperfect. It will be several years before anything like a complete understanding of current economic events is possible. But the severity of the crisis has pushed economics to the top of the public agenda. People who had not previously felt the remotest curiosity about financial matters are now curious, not to say deeply concerned, and want to know more.

We hope here to have answered some of the many questions being asked right now. This is not a comprehensive guide, but an attempt to throw some light on the chain of circumstances that rocked banks and left savers fearing for their financial safety.

We are not writing for bankers and hedge fund managers. They are, of course, welcome to dip in if they think it might help them formulate their investment strategies! But our main aim has been to introduce the sometimes arcane world of finance to the intelligent, non-banking reader.

Hugh Pym and Nick Kochan,
November 2008

1

What happened?

Nationalised banks. The very thought conjures up visions of Labour's election manifesto in 1945 and the demands of street sellers of socialist newspapers. It just was not supposed to happen in the freewheeling world of globalised finance. After all, there is a consensus across political parties that free markets deliver continually rising prosperity and benign outcomes. Rocking the capitalist boat went out of fashion in mainstream politics some time ago.

But it *has* happened, and in the 21st century too. Of all the astonishing developments in the credit crisis which began in August 2007, perhaps the most astonishing is that governments, professing faith in the supremacy of markets, have had to take share stakes in major banks to ensure their survival.

And these were not governments elected on hard left tickets. Who would have believed that Hank Paulson, a Wall Street banker who became George Bush's US Treasury Secretary, would venture to invest state money in such giants as J. P. Morgan and Bank of America? It may have stuck in his craw but he clutched at the idea like a drowning man. And where did the idea come from? New Labour's Gordon Brown who in the recent past had gone out of his way to praise the wealth-generating capabilities of the City of London.

Who would have believed that Royal Bank of Scotland would have the British government as a majority shareholder, and Lloyds-TSB and HBOS would have to tolerate the state as significant minority holders? Bradford and Bingley, carved up by the Treasury and regulators leaving a £40 billion mortgage book on the list of state assets, appears almost a footnote. Northern Rock, which seemed at the time of its rescue by the Bank of England in September 2007 to be one bad apple in an otherwise wholesome basket, is now a distant memory.

Capitalism wobbled. The banking system nearly fell apart. You have to pinch yourself to remember that this was not some sort of bad dream. The financial crisis of 2008 was beyond anyone's worst expectation. You could not have made it up.

'Credit crunch' became a household phrase. People were anxious for knowledge. They fretted over their savings and wondered which banks were safe. Students of early 20th century history scratched their heads and wondered how something which looked and smelt like the Wall Street Crash of 1929 could have developed again. To the average hard-working saver it seemed inconceivable that all the great brains in banks and governments could not prevent the events of the 1920s and 30s being replayed. What about the lessons which had supposedly been learned after the Great Depression?

Penguin rushed out a reprint of the late J. K. Galbraith's classic *The Great Crash 1929*. Writing about Wall Street in 1970, Galbraith describes how people had forgotten the lessons of 1929, fuelling another stock market boom and bust: 'There is merit in keeping alive the memory of those days. For it is neither public regulation nor the improving moral tone of corporate promoters, brokers, bankers, and mutual fund managers which prevents these recurrent outbreaks. It is the recollection of how, on some past occasion, illusion replaced reality and people got rimmed.'

Galbraith was deeply aware of the dangers of unbridled capitalism, but even he might have been surprised if he had survived to see the events of 2007 and 2008 unfold. Once again illusion had replaced reality and people had got rimmed.

Sales of *Das Kapital* by Karl Marx were said to have risen noticeably in Germany. 'Marx is fashionable again,' declared a Berlin publisher, who went on to argue that a new generation of readers had been rattled by the financial crisis and become disillusioned with liberalism. In the *Communist Manifesto*, Marx and his co-author Engels had said one of the essential steps to communism was 'centralisation of credit in the hands of the state'. The bearded guru might have relished capitalism's 21st century crisis.

The events of the credit crisis of the early 21st century were shocking even to those who thought they understood financial markets. The run on Northern Rock and the queues outside branches rocked the confidence of the British financial elite. But they convinced themselves this was an isolated case of bad management. Lessons would be learned, they said.

But a year on, Bear Stearns had been bailed out,

Lehman Brothers had collapsed and Halifax Bank of Scotland had been forced into the arms of Lloyds-TSB. A 40% slump in the Royal Bank of Scotland share price one morning had provoked fears that even the giants of High Street banking might topple. The Governor of the Bank of England, Mervyn King, later admitted the system had been close to collapse. What odds would you have got on that astonishing sequence of events?

Sovereign governments creaked. It emerged that Iceland was on the brink of bankruptcy. How many people understood that this country with 300,000 inhabitants had unleashed a banking leviathan with overseas borrowings five times the nation's economic output? It seemed clever for local authorities and savvy individual savers to chase higher returns with the Icelandic banks. Rather less clever it looked when those banks were reined back in by a despairing Icelandic government, leaving liabilities strewn around the UK.

So how did it happen and could it have been halted in its tracks before the damage got out of hand? These are big questions without simple answers.

The roots of the crisis go some way back into the mists of time. Apportioning blame is hard. Banks, regulators and governments all had a hand in the mistakes. Consumers must also take the stand in the court of expert opinion. They must share responsibility insofar as they were willing buyers of the cheap mortgages and loans that became financial weapons of mass destruction.

More pertinently, could it happen again? People in authority say banking will never be the same. The days of big bonuses and excessive risk-taking are over, they say. Banks must be regulated more vigilantly. But did they not say that in the 1930s and the 1970s? And it still happened again. Maybe fear and greed are built into the DNA of markets – and those who participate in them. Galbraith urges us to keep alive the memory. We can try to do that by telling the story.

Where does the story begin? Perhaps as far back as the 1980s. When Big Bang hit the London stock market, the City was transformed from a cosy club into an international financial centre. London's stockbroking firms had been run as partnerships for generations. They placed orders on behalf of clients. Jobbers, as they were known, were the people on the floor of the Stock Exchange who did the buying and selling. Corporate advisory firms were another distinctive profession in the old City.

Big Bang's reforms, in 1986, abolished the old distinction between broker and jobber. The market went electronic and big financial conglomerates evolved. These brought stock-broking, market-making and corporate finance under one roof. And those conglomerates were predominantly foreign-owned. They could trade across time zones and markets and in almost any financial instrument you would care to name. Globalisation had arrived. London was transformed into a global financial power player, the old-boy network of the City cast aside and forgotten.

As London came into line with New York, international investment banking was propelled to new heights. Major players on the world financial stage could take positions in whatever markets they chose. There were no boundaries for these new powerhouses. Debt could be taken on but then repackaged and sold to others. Risk was spread around the system.

The dot-com bubble saw the international banks at the top of their game. Confident, brash and clever, they traded in as many stocks, bonds and more exotic instruments as they could, as well as advising new internet companies coming to the stock market. Trade in derivatives – that is tradeable securities linked to underlying assets such as mortgages – increased and flourished.

The abolition of the Glass-Steagall Act in 1999 was the symbolic official blessing of these new banking titans. Glass-Steagall had been passed in the aftermath of the Wall Street Crash. It insisted that commercial banks, which took deposits from savers, should be kept insulated from more risky forms of banking. The Act's abolition gave the green light, if one were needed, for giant financial supermarkets to come of age.

As the banks burgeoned, the public appetite for home ownership grew and grew. For bankers this was a market which was too good to miss.

Mrs Thatcher's government in the UK had encouraged people to fulfil their dreams of owning the roof over their heads. Sales of council houses to tenants became a trademark policy of her early years in power.

This policy was supported by Labour after its election victory in 1997. The new government set out its own targets for expanding the percentage of homeowners relative to the total population. This was seen as both politically and economically sound. It was typical of the sort of aspirational Thatcherite policy which Tony Blair and Gordon Brown were disinclined to drop.

Home ownership became part of the American dream too. Significant political support for expanding property ownership evolved in Congress.

But to a much greater extent than in the UK, there was a drive to bring millions of Americans who had never been in a position to afford a mortgage into the housing market. These customers were known in the delicate jargon of the lending industry as 'sub-prime'. Wherever they lived, in trailer parks or rented apartments, and whatever their credit histories, they were ripe to be sold mortgages.

Congress decreed low-income Americans to be a priority market. In 1992, legislators passed laws requiring the government-backed mortgage providers Fannie Mae and Freddie Mac to develop more sub-prime lending. Fannie and Freddie were the pillars of the US housing market. If they indicated they were willing to take more such loans onto their books, banks and other lenders would be incentivised to seek out new customers, safe in the knowledge that the debt could be sold on. By 2008, the two giants had amassed more than half of all the nation's home loans.

The Clinton administration set aggressive targets, with nearly half of all mortgages to be targeted at households with low incomes. The target number for sub-prime loans, defined as loans to borrowers on 60% or less of average earnings, was set at 20% in 2000 to rise to 28% by 2008. It seems strange now that such an ambitious series of goals was set. Why would a government so vigorously promote the idea of owning a home, in effect encouraging low-income families to take on risky levels of debt? But this was the late 1990s and the prospect of another house price crash seemed remote.

Extolling the virtues of owning a house seemed a responsible stance for the administration to take, as well as a politically attractive one. It had its roots in moves by President Jimmy Carter in the late 1970s to open up the mortgage market to ethnic minorities. It is easy with hindsight to ridicule the government's push to expand homeownership, but to many people it seemed to fly in the face of natural justice that those with no credit histories should have to pay higher borrowing costs to get on the housing ladder.

The political drive into sub-prime markets intensified with a row over Fannie and Freddie. In 2004 and 2005, Republicans called for the two giants to be cut down to size and for their dominance of the market to be ended. Fannie and Freddie's management lobbied hard against change. Democrat legislators blocked reform legislation in Congress. They backed Fannie and Freddie's drive to provide yet more funding of the sub-prime market to make home ownership attainable for another swathe of low-income American families.

This persuasive line of argument has been set out by Professor Russell Roberts of George Mason University. He suggests that politicians, both Democrat and Republican, were keen to promote home ownership without using government money. They put pressure on banks and the mortgage providers to ease lending policies in pursuit of social goals. Presidents Clinton and Bush both trumpeted the increase in home ownership levels to record highs. Professor Roberts concludes: 'Beware of trying to do good with other people's money.'

While American politicians demanded more housing-market funding and put pressure on banks and mortgage providers, a new source of cheap finance for the developed economies was on tap. The Chinese economic miracle was throwing off cash at an astonishing rate. The Chinese authorities pegged their currency to the dollar at a conveniently low rate, so their exports swept all before them in North American and European markets. With exports running so far ahead of imports, China ran up huge trade surpluses and more piles of dollars than they knew what to do with. The Chinese authorities looked to reinvest that cash in overseas markets.

Other Asian economies had also piled up savings mountains and needed to disperse them. Local consumers had been scarred by the economic crises of the late 1990s, and were reluctant to spend their cash.

Awash with funding, the Asian banks looked further afield for opportunities to lend it.

In very simple terms, then, the world was awash with money in the early years of the 21st century. Lenders were falling over themselves to find willing borrowers. If the supply of money is outpacing demand, its price will fall. So interest rates came down. It has been estimated (by R. Barrell and A. Choy, in evidence to the House of Commons Treasury Select Committee) that the Chinese trading position was responsible for over half the decline in global interest rates between the late 1990s and the early part of the next decade.

At the same time, even with interest rates low, global inflationary forces were receding. The Asian tigers, tapping their huge pools of cheap labour, churned out cheap goods like clothing and electronics for western markets. Low cost imports, flooding into the developed economies, gave consumers unprecedented bargains. And they proved to be an extraordinarily benign influence on inflation.

Policymakers at the time were focussed on the risks of a major downturn after the bursting of the dot-com bubble. Share prices had tumbled as the internet boom unravelled. Then after 9/11, fears of a slump in the world economy intensified. The United States experienced a short recession. Alan Greenspan, chairman of the US central bank, the Federal Reserve, slashed interest rates to try to keep the economy ticking over in the face of a downturn. His actions were followed in varying degree by other central banks, including the Bank of England.

And so the intriguing cocktail of financial elements which would fuel a lending binge and surge in property prices was shaken up and stirred. Cheap money – and plenty of it – swilled around. Inflation and interest rates were both low, which meant that in real (that is, inflation-adjusted) terms, the cost of borrowing was low.

As banks sought out new lending opportunities, investors became obsessed with finding higher returns. They wanted more than the low interest rates prevailing in the money markets. To use the jargon, there was a 'hunt for yield'. They were ready to push a tidal wave of funding at anyone who wanted to borrow. And if more money is available to borrow, more people will be empowered to buy assets such as houses. So demand for those assets and hence prices can be expected to rise.

Banks and mortgage lenders, encouraged by American politicians, pumped increasing amounts of funding into the housing market. The most fertile new territory was sub-prime. In effect a new market was opening up and there were potentially rich pickings for those lenders who moved in aggressively. Here were borrowers who, because they were deemed to be more risky, could be charged mortgage rates at a chunky premium to rates prevailing in the mainstream mortgage market. The 'yield hunters' charged down this path.

In the ensuing housing market boom, lenders failed to take account of the nature of the risk they were taking on. With property prices apparently rising inexorably, the consequences of default seemed bearable. If a home had to be repossessed it could easily be sold on by the lender. So the higher interest rates charged to sub-prime customers looked like money for old rope.

These more aggressive forms of lending sparked innovations. The traditional retail banking model had seen banks and building societies lend only what they had taken in from savers. Profit came from the predictable, safe and rather dull margin between what borrowers paid and what savers received in interest. But with lower interest rates, persuading new savers to open accounts became harder. New sources of financial liquidity were required.

The wholesale money markets offered a well for new finance. Banks could drop their buckets into these markets and then lend the spoils on to homeowners. To sum up this approach: it was borrowing short, lending long. A mortgage customer might want a five-year fixed-rate mortgage. The bank would agree to that but arrange itself to borrow the money on a shorter time frame, say six months. At the end of that six-month period the bank would negotiate a new source of short-term funding, preferably on better terms. This aggressive management of liabilities was intended to maximise the margin between the rate at which the bank borrowed and the rate charged to the mortgage customer.

The Bank of England estimated that in 2001, British banks were lending roughly the same amount they were taking in deposits. But by the first half of 2008, the surplus of lending over deposits had reached £700 billion. That surplus was funded largely from overseas borrowing by the banks.

At some stage, banks decided that the prosaic process of taking mortgage loans of anything up to 25 years on to their own books was a tad unexciting. Much better, they reasoned, to sell the mortgage to the customer, pocket the fee and then palm it off onto someone else. In that way money could be made without the inconvenience of the loans sitting on the balance sheet, and so falling under the remit of banking regulations. Banks are required to keep funding in reserve at a set percentage of their total loan book.

And so the process of securitisation of mortgages evolved. Loans were bundled up and sold on as packages to the investment community. These so called **asset-backed securities** were in great demand amongst investors on the hunt for yield. They looked secure. After all, they were rooted in a housing market which looked as if it would continue climbing for ever and in which defaults were deceptively low. And they delivered attractive interest rates. Pension funds and hedge funds were among those joining the herd.

Into the bundles of mortgages were tossed sub-prime loans. Nobody asked too many questions about the security of the investment. Demand for the new asset-backed securities gathered momentum, and that in turn fuelled the sub-prime lending frenzy. The tail started to wag the dog as lenders found themselves under pressure to create more sub-prime loans to feed the appetite of the markets.

A more exotic variant was called the CDO (collateralised debt obligation). This consisted of packages of loans of varying risk and with different life-spans. They could include bundled up packages of asset-backed securities. Many contained significant proportions of high-risk loans from the mortgage market.

The banks and their associates who were bundling up the mortgages and securitising them did not believe they were putting any of their shareholders' funds at risk. It was pass the parcel. The loans were handed on so quickly they never appeared on the lenders' balance sheets. And if you are not taking on the risk there is little incentive to analyse it.

Another clever piece of financial chicanery saw potentially risky assets shunted into 'off balance sheet' entities. These were arm's length, ring-fenced devices which would borrow on the money markets and invest in loans and securities. They were called 'special investment vehicles' (SIVs). Their structures were opaque. The banks' shareholders knew little about them even though the banks were underwriting them.

Few experts in the City, never mind ordinary investors, understood SIVs. The leading City investor Anthony Bolton of Fidelity recently revealed he had not heard of them until he came across a small reference in a leading high street bank's annual report and accounts. It was at this point that he decided it was time to sell the group's stake in the bank.

Ratings agencies are supposed to act as checks and balances on the creation of commercial paper (unsecured short-term debt) for investment markets. Their ratings of the creditworthiness of the institutions issuing the paper dictate the level of interest which has to be paid. The better the credit rating, the lower the interest rate – that is the theory at least. At the top of the tree, with AAA ratings, stand governments and leading corporations, such as Microsoft and General Electric. Lower down, but not much, stood the mortgage-backed securities.

These agencies, with the benefit of hindsight, have been criticised for their allegedly lax assessments of mortgage-backed securities. Potential conflicts of interest arose because the ratings agencies earned their keep from the issuers of the securities rather than the investors. They took their fees from the banks which bundled up the investments for sale in the markets. Critics allege that the agencies were too generous in issuing top-notch ratings and did not properly scrutinise what was in the bundles. But the investors who blindly accepted the word of the agencies cannot escape censure.

To use the banking jargon, the pricing of risk went way out of line. In normal times, securities linked to questionable assets would be trading with a high yield interest rate that reflects the risk inherent in them – and certainly at a rate some distance above the safest of paper, like government bonds. But they were not. In other words, investors deluded themselves that that mortgage-backed securities were not really that much less safe than government-backed investments. Alan Greenspan later reflected: 'it was the failure to properly price such risky assets that precipitated the crisis'.

The demand for sub-prime-related mortgage securities gave mortgage lenders a free hand to market loans to anyone who wanted them, and some perhaps who did not. In many cases the borrowers were required to come up with no proof of income. They were not even asked to pay by direct debit from their bank accounts. A cheque in the post would do. When the cheques stopped coming in there was not much anyone could do to keep repayments going.

Some have blamed these lenders for their forceful and sometimes unscrupulous marketing of mortgages on the trailer parks and in the more deprived areas of inner cities. But they were creatures of a system, pawns in a game, with some of the biggest players in world finance calling the shots.

Thus far we have been describing an American drama. But it became an international catastrophe waiting to happen as soon as European and, to a lesser extent, Asian banks started buying the mortgage-backed securities. The parcels were passed way beyond US territory. It has been estimated that more than half the asset-backed securities and CDOs linked to the American mortgage market were offloaded onto foreign banks. HSBC, Barclays and Halifax Bank of Scotland were among the British banking giants who took on board these securities.

The spider's web of liabilities and obligations spun from the US sub-prime mortgage industry was expanded yet further into international markets by means of another piece of financial engineering. Holders of mortgage-backed securities were in theory exposed to the risk of the underlying loans defaulting – that is, the risk that homeowners would not be able to pay their mortgages. But should they wish to offload that risk, a new product was available on the shelf. It was called the credit default swap (CDS). Security holders could buy the CDS as insurance against the default of the underlying mortgages. The issuer of the CDS would take on the risk. And so a new market was created, unregulated, and yet further removed from the original assets. Nobody knew the size. Nobody knew the scale of the exposure or who held it. Nobody liked to ask too many questions.

For the years leading up to the summer of 2007, all these factors created a lending and borrowing bonanza. With so much funding swirling around the markets, a surge in property and other prices was the inevitable consequence. Sure enough, a bubble was inflated and house prices climbed relentlessly. The US housing market led the way, with Britain, Spain and Ireland not far behind. In all four countries the average house price rose by 200%

or more between the mid 1990s and 2007. Some observers claimed that the price rises were closely related to underlying factors such as the shortage of housing supply, but this was tenuous. In reality, the market had cut far adrift from fundamentals.

Household appetite for new debt reached staggering heights. In the UK the ratio of the total stock of borrowing to annual disposable incomes reached £1,700 for every £1,000 earned. This was higher than the US and Spain, two of the most willing borrowing nations and quite a bit more than in France or Germany. Stories of mortgages offered at 120% of the value of homes abounded; so too loan multiples of up to six times a borrower's income.

The cash flowing out from banks to borrowers in the UK often came from foreign lenders. As discussed, mortgages were lent using funds raised on the wholesale money markets as well as savers' deposits, as had traditionally been the case. That funding came as much from the US as homegrown sources. The global credit bubble knew no national boundaries. Overseas investors at this juncture were more than happy to lend to UK plc. It was an economy with a record which they respected and admired.

The stock markets in New York and London took their cue from the boom in the commercial and residential property sector. The long unwinding of the internet bubble had taken shares down remorselessly to reach their low-point just before the Iraq war in March 2003. They had bounced back rapidly, with consumer stocks, buoyed up by rising household demand, among the names on the leader board. Leverage – that is, using borrowed money to invest – was another cylinder in the stock market combustion engine. Hedge funds used loan finance as well as their clients' cash to seek a killing from a rising market.

The rocket fuel of low interest rates was readily available. Central banks had cut the cost of borrowing steadily, apparently unconcerned by the asset bubbles inflating around them. Later, critics would argue that the US Federal Reserve in particular had failed to remove some of the oxygen at an early stage. The Bank of England, when challenged on this point, argue that their remit is consumer price inflation, not asset prices. At this stage the beneficial effects of low cost goods from Asia were being felt and inflation seemed to be heading down below its target. Increasing the cost of credit would squeeze inflation even harder. And the Bank of England could face criticism if it pushed up mortgage costs while inflation was undershooting its target.

As for the regulators, it seemed they had their eyes on the wrong ball. The central banks were aware of the dangers of household debt escalating. But in the UK, regulation of banks no longer came within their remit: it had been transferred to the new Financial Services Authority (FSA). In the Eurozone there was no single cross-border regulator even though banks borrowed across borders. National regulators went with the flow of rising markets, anxious only that they operated competitively. They did not attempt to restrain the banks from excesses which might turn sour.

But generally all seemed set fair. Not many Cassandras could be heard arguing that the reckless behaviour of the banks would inevitably bring doom. There had been some warnings, including one from the Bank for International Settlements, about the dangerous pricing of the mortgage-linked securities. But the debt-fuelled economies seemed set to continue on their upward trajectory. Most banks found themselves unable to step back from issuing loans, for fear of missing out on a continued boom. As Chuck Prince, the Citigroup boss told the *Financial Times*: 'as long as the music is playing, you've got to get up and dance. We're still dancing'. Mr Prince later fell on his sword, one of the first high profile bankers to quit when the credit crisis struck.

The dance stopped on 9 August 2007. At least that is when everybody in the markets and financial media realised there was something terribly wrong. Earlier in the year, though, some of the sharper financial minds had begun to ask questions and discreetly reallocate their investments.

One trader at a leading UK finance house revealed later that he had flown with colleagues to California in early 2007 to take a closer look at the housing market. They had been shocked by the number of unfinished apartment blocks and astonished at the anecdotal evidence of borrowers walking away from their obligations. Taxi drivers told them of falling house prices and showed them boarded up properties. That team of financiers flew home and began offloading their sub-prime positions.

The first clear signal to British investors that all was not well came with an announcement by the biggest UK bank HSBC. Four years before, it had purchased a major US sub-prime lending business called Household. Concerns were raised at the time by campaign groups which argued that a British bank with a high reputation should not be profiting at the expense of financially-stretched American families. Shareholders, meanwhile, were assured this was an exciting deal in a fast-expanding market. By February 2007, however, it was far from exciting. HSBC announced it was writing off nearly £1 billion associated with the investment because of falling house prices and rising levels of foreclosures.

Senior traders at Goldman Sachs decided in the spring of 2007 that the sub-prime party was over. They began covering themselves in the event of a fall, in effect laying bets on prices sliding. It later emerged they had made a £2 billion profit on these bets. By this stage it was clear that the sub-prime market was rocky, evidenced by rising defaults and falling prices. But nobody could foresee the havoc which this tumbling market would wreak on the entire financial system.

By the summer, the markets were getting extremely jittery. The investment bank Bear Stearns announced that two funds specialising in sub-prime debt investments were facing a wave of withdrawals from investors. The ratings agencies

Moodys and Standard & Poor's downgraded thousands of mortgage-backed securities. Investors rushed for the doors, dumping whatever they could. Market prices plummeted.

The penny, or rather the multi-billion-dollar cheque, was dropping. Investors woke up to the truth that property prices can go down as well as up. Clever computer models had rated the mortgage securities after looking back at twenty years' worth of data on housing market defaults. The trouble was that those two decades had been the boom times. The technical experts had ignored or forgotten previous house price slumps.

On 9 August 2007, a leading French bank, BNP Paribas, announced it was suspending three of its investment funds because it was unable to make a sensible valuation of the holdings. In effect it could not pay back investors. The funds' asset-backed securities could not be traded, so it did not know what the funds were worth. There were reports of German banks with similar problems.

Banks began to hoard cash because they feared they might need it to cover losses. This was the liquidity crisis which laid the foundations of the credit crunch. The rates at which banks lend to each other surged, a sign of how nervous they had become about their rivals' solvency. Lending to others was risky if those counterparts were themselves in difficulties.

In the UK, the London Interbank Offered Rate (LIBOR) moved considerably higher than the Bank of England's official rate. This would have significant effects on those mortgage and other household loans linked to LIBOR. The response across the board was to cut lending to anyone, corporate or individual. And so began the tightening of mortgage and other consumer-loan availability which was later to have devastating consequences for the wider economy.

The first casualty was Northern Rock. This former building society had become a bank and floated on the stock market. Ambitious expansion plans saw the Rock pick up larger chunks of the British mortgage market. The directors would later argue in their defence that they had not ventured into sub-prime, either British or American. That was not their problem. What was to become a fatal flaw was their reliance on wholesale markets.

Less than a third of the Rock's business was funded by savers' deposits, the lowest proportion of any UK mortgage lender. The rest had to be raised on the international money markets. That was fine in the good times. But when the money markets froze on 9 August, it became a crippling burden. Almost overnight Northern Rock found itself unable to raise money. Within a month it had limped into the arms of the Bank of England for an emergency loan. The BBC's Robert Peston broke the story and it stunned the financial markets. Images of anxiously queueing depositors outside Northern Rock branches raised eyebrows in Geneva, London and other financial capitals amongst investors who had put their money behind the UK economy.

For many months a blame game was played over Northern Rock. Its directors were vilified for failing to spot the cracks in the edifice they had constructed. They had never dreamed that liquidity could dry up so suddenly. But neither had the regulators. The stress tests they imposed on banks to see how watertight their balance sheets were did not include the seizing up of the money markets. The Financial Services Authority was slated by MPs for this failing.

But Northern Rock was not the last. Other former building societies, which had joined the stock market and the drive to sell more mortgages, faltered. Alliance and Leicester was taken over at a bargain basement price by the Spanish bank Santander, already owner of Abbey. The Spanish group was later to pick up the pieces of Bradford and Bingley.

Her Majesty's government was left owning Northern Rock and the Bradford and Bingley mortgage book.

HBOS was later to falter for the same reason. Its large share of the British mortgage market and the need to raise some of its funding from wholesale markets precipitated a crisis of confidence among investors. They simply did not believe the HBOS business model was sustainable, even for a group with such a leading position in the lending market. By October 2008 a run on its share price had triggered an emergency merger with Lloyds-TSB.

The common thread running through all these cases was that sources of funding which were readily available until the summer of 2007 dried up. Bundling mortgages up into packages and selling them ceased to be viable. It was like removing half the petrol from the country's filling stations. Just as drivers would have to queue at forecourts in such circumstances or take the car home empty, homebuyers now faced queues to obtain mortgages, or the possibility that nothing affordable was available.

And so began a painful process in global financial markets called 'deleveraging'. In simple terms it means cutting your losses. Banks everywhere sought to bail out of high-risk investments, put the brakes on lending and rebuild their reserves. Leading global players announced huge losses as they tried to find appropriate new valuations for their mortgage-based investments, by now branded 'toxic assets'. Scarcely a day would go by without a giant like Citigroup, Merrill Lynch, UBS or Credit Suisse unveiling yet more losses. By October 2008, the Bank of England was to estimate that total losses associated with securitised loans ran to a staggering £1.8 trillion in the US, UK and Eurozone – more than the annual output of the British economy.

The central banks injected ever increasing billions of their currencies into the banking infrastructure in an attempt to reverse the drying up of market liquidity. They provided hard cash or readily tradeable bonds as loans in exchange for mortgage-backed securities and other paper investments as collateral. In other words, they pumped in liquid assets to oil the wheels in return for the banks' unwanted investments. But the Governor of the Bank of

England Mervyn King later argued this was no more than sticking plaster before a longer-term recuperation. What was really needed was new capital.

Capital forms the building blocks of any bank. Regulators do not permit banks to trade unless they have a cushion of cash or high quality bonds which can readily be called on for a rainy day. If big losses are run up, capital has to be used to plug the gaps. In these circumstances it will ebb away fast.

By early 2008 the banks had realised they were short of capital. Those most in need bit the bullet and went to the stock market to raise it. In the case of Royal Bank of Scotland, shareholders were asked to stump up an eye-watering £12 billion. This, in City parlance, is known as a 'rights issue'. Existing shareholders are given the right to buy new shares at a discounted price. Big institutions, in return for a fee, act as underwriters and pick up any of the new shares not wanted by the shareholders. Rights issues are sometimes seen as an admission of failure, with the company having to go cap in hand to its shareholders. Even more so when £12 billion is needed for the cap. Sir Fred Goodwin, at RBS, was living on borrowed time after that.

In the summer of 2008, Bear Stearns had been bailed out in the United States on the orders of the Treasury Secretary Hank Paulson, but there was a feeling in some quarters that the worst might be over. Interbank lending rates fell, suggesting that strains were easing. Some mortgage lenders came up with more competitive fixed-rate deals. But the events of September 2008 were to shatter that complacency.

First, Fannie and Freddie were, in effect, nationalised. This ended confusion as to the precise nature of the American government guarantees. But it rekindled fears in the markets as to the ability of the US mortgage market to operate in anything like normal circumstances. Then came the shock news that Lehman Brothers was to be allowed to fail. Paulson decided to make an example of the once shining star of the investment banking world and leave it to the not so tender mercy of market forces.

Images of bankers leaving Lehman Brothers' offices in New York and London with their possessions in cardboard boxes shocked the financial world. The threat of redundancies was bad enough. But the bigger worry was the massive scale of losses which those who had traded with Lehmans now faced. The giant insurer AIG was a casualty within days. It had to be bailed out by the US government because of its heavy involvement in credit default swaps and the insurance of stricken bonds.

The Lehmans collapse triggered the next act of the banking drama. Any investor who had been minded to buy bonds or securities issued by banks had now been scared off. Now that the authorities had shown themselves prepared to see a bank fail, rendering those investments worthless, the risks had escalated.

All this coincided with the growing realisation that banks' capital reserves, even after cash-raising exercises, were inadequate. The US housing market had continued to slide, mortgage-related investments were still falling in value and the scale of future losses was only likely to rise. Banks became even less willing to lend and the interbank rate soared again.

Hank Paulson and the American administration came up with their $700 billion bailout plan. It was nearly derailed by a Congress unhappy with the idea of rescuing Wall Street bankers. In the UK, meanwhile, in one ghastly 48-hour period, on 6 and 7 October, the share prices of leading banks, led by RBS, fell off a cliff. Investors feared that the banks would be unable to tap new money in the wholesale market. Senior City sources later admitted the banking system was close to running out of cash. It was the British government's turn to intervene with its own recapitalisation plan.

The use of taxpayers' money to provide banking capital was just the latest astonishing twist in a dramatic story. The financial world had been turned on its head. Recapitalisation, some felt, might just draw a line under the banking crisis, leaving the main players to lick their wounds and continue the painful process of rebuilding. But it looked to others as if it might just be the opening scene in a drama whose next act would be a sharp and potentially agonising world recession.

2

What is being done?

What is being done about the crisis?

The measures being taken by governments around the world aim to address two separate issues: solvency and liquidity.

Solvency refers to the ability of institutions – in this case banks and other financial insitutions – to pay their debts in a timely manner. Because many assets held by these institutions have proved to be worth far less than was previously believed (i.e. asset-backed securities), as well as less easily 'liquidated' (converted into cash), such institutions have found themselves under severe financial pressure. In some cases they have found themselves unable to remain solvent. Governments have tried to remedy this by providing fresh capital: that is, they have used taxpayers' money to buy shares in banks and other struggling financial institutions.

Liquidity refers to the overall state of a market rather than to the state of individual players. A liquid market has ready and willing buyers and sellers at all times. There has been a crisis of liquidity because trust has evaporated in the value of some key financial instruments, in particular those linked to mortgages. As a result, banks and other financial institutions are hoarding cash, both to cover their own potential and actual losses and because they are nervous about lending to other institutions which may find themselves unable to repay the debt on time.

Central banks and governments around the world are

attempting to revive liquidity in various ways. They have reduced interest rates to make borrowing cheaper. In some cases, they have offered to swap vast amounts of illiquid, non-tradeable instruments (i.e. securities related to sub-prime mortgages) for more easily cashable bills. And in an effort to restore confidence, they are guaranteeing large sums of the banks' borrowing on the money markets.

In several countries, governments have moved to prevent a 'run' on banks by offering varying levels of guarantee on savers' deposits.

'Not since the First World War has our banking system been so close to collapse. The long march to boredom and stability starts tonight.'

Mervyn King, Governor of the Bank of England

What measures is the UK government taking?

The government is pumping very large sums, up to a total of £50 billion, into financial institutions that require capital to continue normal operations. To put this figure in context, the government spends around £75 billion per year on the National Health Service. In return, the government is taking shares in these institutions. Some of the shares are preference shares; others are ordinary shares. Preference shares take priority over ordinary shares in the paying out of dividends.

In order to free up the money markets and create liquidity, the government is guaranteeing up to £250 billion of the banks' borrowing in these markets. This will not necessarily entail actual expenditure, since the government is merely acting as guarantor rather than supplying the money. It will only have to pay out if some of the guaranteed debt turns out to be 'bad'.

As part of its 'special liquidity scheme', the Bank of England is releasing £200 billion of funding onto the money markets, by swapping government-backed bills for difficult-to-trade, toxic securities. The aim, again, is to 'unfreeze' inter-bank lending. The Bank of England has also reduced interest rates, hoping that this cut will trickle through to the wider economy and help to release credit.

Finally, the government has guaranteed individual savings deposits of up to £50,000 in any one account. This is to bolster savers' confidence and prevent a run on the banks.

Where is all the money for the rescue coming from?

The government has gone to the capital markets to borrow the money it needs for the bailout. It does this by issuing bonds, a form of IOU. UK government bonds are known as gilts, an abbreviation of 'gilt-edged'. The debt that the government accrues by issuing these gilts adds to the National Debt. Like every other borrower, the government has to pay interest to its lenders, but owing to the very small perceived risk that it will default (that is, fail to pay its debts on time), the government is able to borrow at a relatively low rate of interest.

Governments are able to borrow money on the capital markets more easily and cheaply than banks because it is extremely rare for a western government to default on its repayments. This is because governments (provided they are operating in a lawful environment) are in the privileged position of being able to raise taxes to pay their debts. No other borrower can boast a comparably easy way of generating cash.

Ironically, many of the institutions buying the government gilts required to keep the British banks afloat are the British banks themselves. Other gilt purchasers are financial institutions like insurance companies and international investors, not to mention Sovereign Wealth Funds belonging to super-rich states like those in the Gulf.

What strings are attached to the government's rescue of the banks?

The government has laid down several conditions. Senior staff in the banks that have chosen to participate in the scheme are prohibited from paying themselves cash bonuses over the course of the coming year. Any bonuses they receive must be in the form of shares. They will therefore be rewarded only if their institution prospers and if this is reflected in the share price.

The banks are also prohibited from paying their shareholders a dividend until they have redeemed the government's preference shares. Some banks are contesting this, not without good reason. A number of large institutional investors depend on dividends to pay out guaranteed returns. The ban on dividends has caused these powerful funds to sell bank shares, which partly explains why share prices have fallen since the scheme was announced.

The government has stated that it wants bank lending to home owners and small businesses to return to the levels that preceded the credit crunch in mid-2007. However, it is not clear how this condition will be enforced, and banks are showing signs of reluctance to comply.

Finally, the government will be represented on the boards of the banks in which it has bought ordinary shares.

Are all banks eligible for government support?

The government has created the term 'eligible institution' to describe those banks that qualify for the bailout. An eligible institution is a bank or other financial institution which has a significant presence in the wholesale money markets and is important to the national economy. Non-British-owned institutions operating in the UK such as Abbey National, which is controlled by the Spanish bank Santander, do qualify for the bailout. Not all eligible institutions are banks. For instance, the Nationwide Building Society is an eligible institution because of its importance to the economy.

'We are in the midst of a once-in-a-century credit tsumani. Those of us who have looked to the self-interest of lending institutions to protect shareholders' equity are in a state of shocked disbelief.'

Alan Greenspan

Have all banks accepted government support?

No. Although most large financial institutions are eligible, some have chosen to decline the government's offer of help.

For instance, HSBC, the UK's largest bank, has opted out of the rescue operation. HSBC took a quick and decisive response to its multi-billion-pound sub-prime losses, writing off these toxic assets and thereby demonstrating to the market that it did not have a solvency issue (i.e. had sufficient capital reserves to absorb the losses).

Barclays Bank also stayed outside the government's bailout, in their case by tapping private investors for £7 billion of new capital. The bulk of this, around £5.8 billion, came from two Middle Eastern sources: from Qatar Holding and Challenger, controlled by Sheikh Hamad Bin Jabr Al-Thani, and from Sheikh Mansour Bin Zayed Al Nahyan, a member of Abu Dhabi's ruling family. The deal caused some controversy, with many of Barclays' existing shareholders feeling that the cost of avoiding government intervention was too high: in other words, that the incoming investors had been given too good a deal. Some have suggested that Barclays' senior management might have been motivated as much by their desire to continue to receive cash bonuses (which are disallowed under the terms of the government bailout) as by a consideration of their shareholders' best interests.

Do the banks have to repay the government?

The government's investment in the banks is in the form of ordinary shares and preference shares.

The banks have to pay interest at 12% to the government on the preference shares. They must also 'redeem' (repay) the preference shares in full at some point in the future. Those banks in which the government has taken preference shares have a strong incentive to redeem them as soon as they can, not only because they are expensive (they have a high rate of interest) but also because the banks are not allowed to pay a dividend to their ordinary shareholders until they have done so.

The ordinary shares are an equity investment and therefore not repayable. The government is free to cash its investment by selling its shares on the open market. Depending on the performance of the banks in the coming months and years, the government – and the taxpayer – may make either a profit or a loss on this investment.

Are the banks really being nationalised?

Yes. Several banks have been partly nationalised, or brought under state ownership. The government holds a majority stake in Royal Bank of Scotland and significant minority stakes in Lloyds-TSB and HBOS, among others. And let's not forget Northern Rock, nationalised early on in the crisis. However, the word can be misleading, and there are big differences between the nationalisations of the post-war Labour government and those occurring today.

The post-war Labour government was ideologically committed to widening state control of the 'commanding heights' of the economy, such as the coal and steel industries. To this end it compelled private owners within these industries to sell them their companies. More recently, the French and Venezuelan governments have pursued similar policies.

The rescue of the banks carried out by the government in late 2008 has been motivated by pragmatic rather than ideological considerations. It is the government's explicit policy to maintain stability in the financial system. The banks came to the government asking for support, arguing that without such support their survival would be put at risk, with devastating repercussions for the economy as a whole.

What control will the government have over how these nationalised banks are run?

Considerable control. In addition to the above-mentioned conditions attached to the bailout, the government will appoint members to the banks' boards. The Board of Directors of a company is the body responsible for top-level decision-making. The exact degree of influence that the government will be able to exert depends on the composition of the bank boards. The government will not have a majority on any board, and has made assurances that it is broadly committed to preserving the banks' commercial independence and maintaining an 'arm's-length' relationship. The banks themselves have also been keen to downplay the level of government interference.

The government is creating a new agency, UK Financial Investments Ltd, specifically to manage its holdings in the banking sector. The agency will be a part of the Treasury and will be separate from the Shareholder Executive, which currently manages holdings in UK companies on behalf of the government. Its remit, according to the Chancellor Alistair Darling, is to 'protect and create value for the taxpayer as a shareholder'.

Is the plan to de-nationalise the banks again in the future? When?

The government has stated that it has no intention to hold on to the bank shares any longer than it has to, and that it expects to return the banks to the private sector in the next three years. However, this is not a binding commitment, and the government is free to retain ownership of its shares for as long as it wishes.

The government has raised the money it is investing in the banks by issuing three-to-five-year gilts. It may therefore be assumed that it is expecting to cash its investment within three to five years, so that it will be able to repay the money it has borrowed.

Of course, it is possible that the government will not be able to recover all the money it has invested in ailing financial institutions within this time-frame. Like any other investor, it runs the risk that the value of its shares will fall. In this case it may either sell at a loss or hold on to the shares in the hope that they will rise again in the future.

There is also the risk that the banks in which the British taxpayer has invested will go bust, although the events of late 2008 show how reluctant the government is to let this happen.

When was the last time the government was forced to nationalise large companies, and what happened?

When the British government nationalised the ailing motor company British Leyland in 1975, there was a comparable uproar. This was also a rescue measure rather than the ideological pursuit of a policy of state ownership. In the event, the company was no more successful under state control than it had been in the private sector. Nevertheless, it remained in government hands for eleven years before being returned to private control. It was then broken up and sold off to many other parties. The case of British Leyland bears little relationship to what is occurring now with UK banks, which are integral to the functioning of the UK economy and therefore cannot so easily be allowed to go bust.

'The theory of Communism may be summed up in one sentence: abolish all private property.'

Karl Marx

Why is the government guaranteeing personal savings?

This guarantee is designed to give depositors total confidence that they will receive back their deposits should their bank or building society fail.

The protection of the banking system via a guarantee on personal savings makes sense in terms of larger economic policy. If there were a widespread loss of confidence in banks, causing savers to withdraw their money *en masse*, normal economic activity would be drastically impaired. In a market economy, the banks perform the vital function of intermediation: that is, they borrow from depositors, and lend to people who want to invest, in a business, in property, and so on. If the banks didn't exist, that key function would not be performed, and there would be no such thing as a market economy. All financial intermediation would have to be done by the government, as it is in communist economies.

However, the government's 'guarantee' is not quite as copper-bottomed as some believe. There is no legal guarantee of more than £50,000 of personal savings in any one account, although the Chancellor of the Exchequer has said that he will ensure that no individual depositor loses money as a result of a bank failure. The potential cost of guaranteeing all individual savings is £5.2 trillion – or roughly four times GDP.

How come the banks are still paying large bonuses?

Under the terms of the bailout, banks that have accepted money from the government are prohibited from paying their management cash bonuses, but they are still free to pay out bonuses in shares.

Banks such as Barclays and HSBC that have not entered the scheme retain complete control over what and how they pay their executives. Barclays has stated that it did not accept the bailout in order to avoid government intervention and retain control of its policies. Some have suggested that the senior management's wish to continue to pay themselves cash bonuses was a factor in this decision.

There is a potential breach of contract where, prior to the bailout, banks had already made a commitment to pay cash bonuses, and banks are having to examine their legal obligations. It is possible that executives deprived of the bonuses they were promised will bring lawsuits against their employers. In that case, it would be up to the courts to decide the outcome.

What might happen if several banks went bust?

This could only occur as a result of severe negligence by the powers that be, and so far they have proved very alert to the risk. However, it is worth pointing out that banks are different from most other companies because of systemic risk: the risk that, if one fails, others are likely to follow. This is not true of publishing houses or football clubs.

Multiple bank failures would cause extreme panic. People would be unable to access their money, and therefore to purchase basic goods – assuming these were available in the shops, since businesses would be unable to pay their suppliers, who might then refuse to supply. About 40% of food consumed in the UK is imported, so severe food shortages could result if the pound were to collapse and importers found themselves unable to afford to pay for goods. In order to avoid mass starvation, the government would be forced to take over the British food industry and use its own cash reserves (or, more likely, raise more money) to pay for imports.

However, this scenario is very unlikely. As we have seen, the government is prepared to go to great lengths (i.e. nationalising banks) to protect the country's financial system from meltdown.

Have rules about competition been waived to allow recent mergers to go through?

Yes. The government has driven a coach and horses through established rules on market share.

The merger of Lloyds-TSB and Halifax Bank of Scotland (HBOS) will produce a leviathan with a 30% share of retail and mortgage markets. HBOS has a number of mortgage brands under its umbrella, including Halifax, Intelligent Finance, Bank of Scotland and Birmingham Midshires. It will also be the biggest player in life insurance, with some 18% of the market. Lloyds-TSB itself has the Cheltenham and Gloucester mortgage operation.

The Office of Fair Trading (OFT), charged by the Competition Commission with examining mergers where there is a risk that the joint market share of both parties will exceed 25%, concluded: 'There is a realistic prospect that the anticipated merger will result in a substantial lessening of competition in relation to personal current accounts, banking services for small and medium-sized enterprises and mortgages'.

However, the government overruled a referral to the Competition Commission on the grounds that it had a 'serious concern about public interest'. A long-term reduction in consumer choice in the retail banking and mortgage sectors therefore looks likely to be a further consequence of the credit crunch.

How confident can we be that the government's measures will work?

The government's measures aim to resolve the solvency and liquidity crises in the financial sector: in other words, to prevent banks from going bust, and to stop the flow of money through the economy from drying up. At the time of writing, no major banks have collapsed, and liquidity has been slowly increasing. The government hopes the flow of credit will return to the levels that existed before the crisis began in 2007, but many experts believe this is beyond the scope of its interventions.

It is too early to take a view on whether the government's actions will be sufficient to restore health to the economy in the medium term. Share prices fell dramatically when the bailout was announced. This may have been due to a fear among investors that it would be inadequate to prevent further problems in the financial sector.

There are also many potentially serious problems in the pipeline that the bailout does not address. Sectors that have hitherto escaped relatively unscathed, such as insurance and pensions, may get into difficulties. At this stage, it appears that the recapitalisation of the banks may have stopped the rot.

What is the US government doing?

The US government is adopting a similar strategy to the UK government, designed to ensure the solvency of the country's major financial institutions, and to restore liquidity to the system.

The two biggest lenders in the US mortgage market, Freddie Mae and Fannie Mac, have been nationalised, along with AIG, the world's biggest insurance company. Many other major banks have received capital injections from the US Treasury.

The government has also given deposit insurance to trillions of dollars of money market funds. In mid-November 2008, Treasury Secretary Hank Paulson reversed his controversial decision to purchase $700 billion of toxic mortgage-related assets. Paulson said the money would be better spent on recapitalising banks and supporting markets that securitise consumer credit. This is a dramatic about-turn on a policy that was at the core of the American 'Troubled Asset Relief Programme' (TARP).

The US bank rescue package differs from that adopted in the UK in one important respect. Whereas UK institutions have the choice whether to accept the government money (and some have opted to decline it) nine leading US banks have no such choice.

How are different countries collaborating?

Countries are collaborating under the aegis of organisations like the European Central Bank, the International Monetary Fund and the Bank for International Settlements.

Central banks have also been working together in unprecedented ways. On 8 October 2008, the Federal Reserve, the Bank of England and the European Central Bank announced co-ordinated cuts in lending rates, with most trimming by half a percentage point.

However, the issue of collaboration is complicated by each country's pursuit of different problems and different policy objectives. This was starkly demonstrated when the government of Ireland departed from the herd and gave depositors a full guarantee covering any amount of funds. This triggered a welcome flow of funds to Irish banks, but put pressure on other countries to provide their own deposit guarantee schemes. Ireland attracted much criticism in the wake of this decision.

3

How will the crisis affect me?

Is there going to be a recession?

An economy enters recession when its gross domestic product (GDP) contracts over two successive quarters. The first indication that the UK would meet this criterion appeared on 23 October 2008 when data were released showing that GDP in the third quarter of 2008 had contracted by 0.5%. The economy is universally expected to meet the technical definition of a recession in January 2009 when the figures for GDP in the fourth quarter of 2008 are released.

Some economists were warning of a mild UK recession as early as the middle of 2007. They had read the runes of rising inflation, a weakening housing market, falling company profits and liquidity problems in the financial markets, and concluded that the UK economy was under severe pressure. Indeed the Chancellor of the Exchequer himself, while on holiday in Scotland in August 2008, told a journalist that the economy was at its weakest for sixty years.

The Governor of the Bank of England and the Prime Minister first publicly uttered the dreaded 'R' word in the middle of October 2008 to prepare the country for tough times ahead. This was a particularly difficult moment for Prime Minister Gordon Brown who, as Chancellor of the Exchequer for ten years, had claimed to preside over the end of the cycle of 'boom and bust'.

Is the credit crunch to blame for the recession?

The credit crunch is not the sole cause of the economic downturn, but it is certainly a contributory factor. Rising prices in commodities like oil and food had already sapped people's ability to buy other goods. A falling housing market had also started to affect consumer spending, since people were no longer able to draw ever greater sums of money against their houses to fund their purchases on the high street and in the retail park.

The sudden reduction of available credit dramatically worsened the economic situation. Businesses found themselves unable to obtain from banks the cash they needed to maintain existing levels of activity, or indeed solvency. As a result, the number of bankruptcies increased, and staff have been laid off in an attempt to cut costs. In turn, rising unemployment has placed further pressure on businesses selling goods or services to consumers, by reducing the amount of cash those consumers have available to spend.

How long will a recession last?

It is much too early to give any definite view on this, and estimates range widely.

Some economists argue that the authorities took sufficiently swift and decisive action to prevent the financial system from melting down and causing long-term damage. They expect the recession to be shallow and short, with two quarters of negative growth followed by a slow but steady revival in economic activity.

More pessimistic commentators expect a grinding recession lasting several years. They point to Japan's recent history as a sobering lesson in how intractable the problems that now face the UK economy could be. In the early nineties, Japan suffered a similarly deflating asset-price bubble, which also led to a financial crisis and a drying-up of credit. The Japanese economy remained stagnant for fifteen years, and has been kept ticking over only by massive government borrowing, increasing the national deficit to colossal proportions – currently more than 1.5 times the country's GDP.

As in Japan, the UK banking sector will need time to rebuild its balance sheets and accumulate capital after the huge losses it has endured. Only once banks have done this can they safely begin lending again.

How similar is the economic situation now to the one in the early nineties?

Between 1991 and the end of 1992, the British economy contracted over six quarters. A bursting housing bubble was a factor then as now, and house prices fell substantially during this period, putting many people into negative equity. This is when the sum borrowed against an asset such as a house is greater than the market value of the asset itself. Negative equity does not in itself create a problem, provided the homeowner can afford to keep up payments on his mortgage and does not need to move home. But it can be ruinous and lead to bankruptcy if for any reason there is a need to move – perhaps owing to redundancy or other loss of income.

House prices are falling more rapidly now than they did in the early nineties. And although a credit boom did precede the last recession, today's levels of personal debt are far higher, amounting to an eye-popping £1.44 trillion, or 1.7 times the average household's annual disposable income. However, interest rates are currently lower, so this debt is currently less expensive to service.

One significant difference is that the last economic downturn was not accompanied by a banking crisis, with the consequent massive government expenditure on the rescue package.

Are people's savings really at risk?

Most individual savings accounts are not at risk. Those who have their money in UK banks are covered by the government's guarantee of up to £50,000 in any one account. In addition to this formal guarantee, the Chancellor has issued a promise that no depositor in these banks will lose any money. This is not binding, but the political cost of reneging on it would be severe. Individuals with accounts in several insolvent Icelandic banks have also received a guarantee from the Chancellor that they will receive their money back.

By way of historical comparison, the biggest recent banking failure in the UK involved the Bank of Credit and Commerce International. This was closed down in 1991 following the discovery of massive fraud. In the event, the major shareholder, the Sheikh of Abu Dhabi, came to the rescue of depositors, who ended up receiving back most of their money. Prior to this, in 1984, the banking arm of Johnson Matthey found itself insolvent, having made a number of high-risk loans which turned out to be of dubious quality. To forestall a wider banking crisis, the Bank of England organised a rescue package, involving the purchase of the bank for £1.

What can people do to minimise the risk of losing their savings?

In light of the government's guarantee of £50,000 for each individual deposit, one way of reducing risk is to keep no more than this amount in any one bank or building society. Those lucky enough to have very large cash savings will therefore need to open as many accounts with different banks and building societies as their funds dictate.

People may wish to diversify further and avoid complete reliance on the banking system by putting their savings into government securities, government-backed National Savings and Investment (NS&I) schemes, or commodities such as gold. However, these options lack the convenience of banks, which not only pay interest on savings, but enable the saver to access their money at a moment's notice.

'The man who will live above his present circumstances, is in great danger of soon living beneath them.'

Joseph Addison

What is the difference between a building society and a bank?

Building societies are mutual institutions, which means they are owned by their members. They provide a full banking service without making a profit. All customers become members, but do not receive dividends.

Building societies are important providers of mortgages. The Nationwide, for example, is one of the country's largest mortgage and financial institutions, with a market share of around 10% of all mortgage lending.

Building societies have been much less exposed to the credit crunch than banks. While some have borrowed in the wholesale markets to finance their lending – and so have been exposed to the liquidity freeze that has hit banks – most have lent from deposits placed by their members.

The banks, on the other hand, borrowed heavily on the wholesale capital markets and were left high and dry when that source of money dried up as a result of a general loss of confidence among lenders.

Over the last twenty years many building societies have turned themselves into banks, in a process called 'demutualisation'. Demutualised building societies, most notoriously Northern Rock, tended to borrow aggressively on the money markets to maximise profits. In consequence they have been severely hit by the collapse of those markets.

Is there a connection between a bank's share price and its ability to refund depositors?

The share price gives an indication of a bank's strength, by providing a measure of the profits investors expect the company to make in the future. Its reliability as a measure of a bank's solvency depends on the accuracy of these expectations, which in turn depends partly on the quality of the information available. In the latter part of 2008, bank share prices fluctuated erratically, as investors struggled to make any sense of the rapidly changing economic and business environment.

Although they should not be viewed uncritically, movements in a bank's share price relative to the sector are probably as good an indication as anything else of its solvency. Depositors may also look to the bank's credit rating to provide clues, although these ratings have proved of dubious merit in the run-up to these turbulent economic conditions.

How might nationalisation affect people's experience of their banks in the high street?

Ordinary day-to-day business with a bank will not be affected. The government is just another shareholder and is not likely to try to change basic banking services. The only people who might notice a change as a result of the rescue scheme are those who are looking for credit for their small business or to buy a house. If banks play by the rules set by the government, which stipulate that they should maintain 'competitively-priced lending to homeowners and to small businesses at 2007 levels', they will look more favourably on these requests. However, banks are so far robustly resisting government pressure to release credit and are likely to continue to do so while their sources of finance in the wholesale money markets remain so expensive, and while they remain short of essential capital. Indeed, the Council of Mortgage Lenders has questioned whether a return to 2007 levels of lending would be 'either prudent or desirable'.

Is the cost of ordinary goods going to rise?

Most economists agree that prices are likely to fall rather than rise as the country enters recession. This is because people will have less money to buy goods so retailers will be forced to lower their prices to maintain sales. Falls in commodity prices like wheat, oil and rice, knocked by the global shortage of money, will also exert a downward pressure on prices. The greater risk may actually be deflation – when the price of ordinary goods falls – as occurred in Japan through the 1990s. Deflation, once entrenched, is difficult to cure, as the economist J. M. Keynes recognised back in the 1930s.

However, there may be some inflationary pressures in the mix. Trade unions may seek large pay rises to compensate for the price increases of the last year. This will put more money in pockets, which may help shops and service providers avoid slashing their prices.

The exchange rate is another factor. If the pound falls against foreign currencies, as it did precipitately in mid-October, importers will need to pay more for goods made abroad. These added costs may be reflected in prices in British shops.

Are taxes going to rise?

Taxes are very unlikely to rise in the next two or three years, as the government will be keen to keep money in people's pockets so they can buy goods and services. Low taxation will help encourage consumers to spend money at a time when recession is making them feel worried about their jobs and the value of their houses.

In addition to fiscal stimulus in the form of low taxation, the government has other options at its disposal to boost consumer spending and kick-start the economy. For example, it can raise money on the domestic and international markets (thereby increasing the **National Debt**) in order to finance a programme of public works, where the unemployed become employed to work on specific projects for the state. The UK government's current programme of constructing social housing is designed partly to fulfil this purpose.

Government spending in times of economic stagnation was advocated in the 1930s by John Maynard Keynes, the distinguished English economist, in his ground-breaking book, *The General Theory of Employment, Interest and Money*.

What are the main factors affecting house prices?

Many factors affect the housing market. An important factor at present is the scarcity of bank credit available to house buyers. If this were the sole or the main influence, it might be reasonable to conclude that house prices will revive if the government's current efforts to persuade banks to renew their lending to would-be borrowers are successful.

However, there are other forces in play. For example, it is widely believed that a bubble in house prices was inflated in the decade up to 2007: in other words, that prices rose to unsustainable levels relative to incomes. It is claimed that during this period, many people, far from repaying their mortgages, were borrowing more and more against the rising value of their home.

If this proves to be the case and house prices had indeed reached fundamentally unsustainable highs, an easing in credit conditions will have little effect until prices fall to levels that are more affordable in the long term.

Are house prices going to fall?

Whatever estate agents and other interested parties say, there is little reason to believe that the current trend will change in the short term. Both purchasers and sellers are finding the market unattractive. Purchasers are unable to obtain the credit from banks or building societies to pay house prices at current levels, and may also be holding back in the expectation that prices will fall even further. Sellers are being deterred by the shortage of buyers and the belief that their house will soon rise again in value to what it was at the peak of the market. Additionally, home owners with negative equity may not be able to afford to sell and take the loss.

House prices dropped by 8% in the year to September 2008, according to the UK Land Registry. Expert forecasts for the next year vary, but this may accelerate to 15% year-on-year, as the recession bites. With inflation factored in, the annual drop in real house prices could reach 20%. This is much sharper than at the end of the last boom in house prices.

However, the housing market could be cushioned from even more drastic falls by a reduction of mortgage rates in the short-to-medium term, although these rates are not likely to fall in line with Bank of England base rate. The cost of borrowing on the inter-bank market remains high, and mortgage lenders are trying to resist government pressure to pass the reductions in the official rate on to borrowers.

How safe are pensions now?

There are many different kinds of pensions, of varying levels of security.

Most private pensions depend largely on the perform-ance of their investments in the financial markets. If the financial markets are performing badly, these pensions will be adversely affected.

There are several ways in which holders of pensions can reduce their exposure to stock market movements. One way is to switch to a pension with a smaller component of equity investment. Such pensions have a smaller 'upside' but compensate by a lower risk of falling in value.

Some private pensions carry guarantees of a certain level of return, often based on a proportion of the holder's final salary. In recent years, these have become less widespread, and even before the crisis fewer than one in five employers still had a final, salary-based pension scheme open to new members of staff. This type of pension is likely to become rarer still.

The government currently guarantees the retirement income of those who have private pensions with companies that have gone out of business.

Is unemployment going to rise?

Yes. Companies under financial pressure will be forced to reduce their headcount as a swift means of reducing that pressure. This will not be sufficient to save some of these companies and many will go bust, causing further job losses. A considerable rise in unemployment seems inevitable, with some economists forecasting that two million people will be out of work by the end of this year and up to three million by the end of next year.

Some vacancies may be created for unemployed British workers by migrant workers returning to their home countries in Central and Eastern Europe to take advantage of improving economic conditions there. It is likely that the government will also try to create jobs though publicly funded projects.

A recession would differ from others in terms of the industries that shed staff. Whereas in previous slumps the brunt has been borne by industrial workers laid off by companies cutting back on production, this time round the jobless will come largely from white-collar sectors of the economy. This reflects the decline in the importance of the manufacturing sector to the UK economy, and the growing proportion of GDP that is contributed by service sectors like finance, tourism, media and real estate.

Which are the safest jobs during a recession?

The beneficiaries of a weakening economy gripped in the vice of recession are rather few. Liquidators, a branch of the accounting profession, will certainly be in demand as company bankruptcies rise. There will also be a demand for lawyers in the City of London to pursue actions against banks alleged to have mis-sold asset-backed securities.

Public-sector workers are also unlikely to be laid off in large numbers, both for political and economic reasons. Politically, the government will not want to be seen to be contributing to rising unemployment. Economically, it will want to do everything within its power to keep people earning salaries and therefore spending money. Indeed, it is possible that the number of public sector jobs will rise over the course of the recession, as the government tries to spend its way out of trouble.

Is the stock market going to fall further?

The trillion-dollar question! And one, of course, that is impossible to answer with any degree of confidence.

The value of a stock at any one time reflects the pooled views of all investors, on the basis of the information available, as to the value (and likely future value) of the company in question. Anyone trying to predict which way the stock will move next should bear in mind that consistent success depends on being wiser than the herd. Most of this herd (it is perhaps worth remembering) are professional investors.

'In the business world, the rearview mirror is always clearer than the windshield.'

Warren Buffett

Is gold a safe investment?

Gold has been regarded as a store of value for many millennia. Until the early 20th century, monetary policy was based on a 'gold standard' which underpinned the value of money. Today, investors still tend to regard gold as a safe haven in times of political and economic uncertainty.

However, like any other investment, gold is subject to the vagaries of investor sentiment. In the weeks after the crisis took hold, this was reflected in its dramatically fluctuating price, which peaked at $918 an ounce on 9 October 2008 before collapsing, along with the stock markets, to $717 an ounce on 13 November 2008.

Compared with shares in a company, investing in gold is relatively safe. In the absence of an unforeseeable change in the laws of physics, gold will not suddenly cease to exist, as a bankrupt company can. But as Karl Marx pointed out in the 19th century, gold has very limited commercial or industrial use. Its value therefore depends on people continuing to find it desirable. Since gold has been coveted by our species throughout its history, from the Aztecs to the Ancient Egyptians to the 21st century New Russians, some may conclude that the situation is unlikely to change now.

4

What is happening in the rest of the world?

Is this a global crisis?

The crisis has its roots in the US housing market, but the repercussions of the bursting of that bubble are now being felt around the world. Banks in Europe have failed, Hungary and the Ukraine have had to turn to the IMF for help and much of the developed world is already in recession. So this is a truly global crisis. No economy in the world will survive unaffected.

But not every country will suffer equally. Britain, for example, might suffer more than most, since households here are more indebted and house prices are more inflated relative to incomes than in many other countries. A collapse in house prices and the attempt by households to reduce their debt will have repercussions for the real economy – the economy which employs people who make things or provide a service. This is already happening. Output in Britain has begun to contract, as it has in Spain and Ireland.

Other countries may fare better. Some of the recently successful emerging markets such as China may simply see a slowdown in their growth rates rather than a outright contraction. That, and the collapse in commodity and food prices that is predicted to accompany the recession, offers a faint ray of hope. As a result, inflation should fall. This will make the policy task of combatting recession easier, leaving central banks more room to cut interest rates in order to stimulate a revival of economic activity.

What makes a currency 'strong' or 'weak'?

A currency is 'strong' when its price rises versus other currencies, and 'weak' when it falls. Like the price of anything else, a currency's price depends on supply and demand.

In the short term, speculation on exchange rates is an important influence on the supply and demand of a currency. When in 1992 the financier George Soros bet against the pound, the world market was flooded with sterling and the price fell dramatically.

Interest rates are also important. High interest rates stimulate demand for a currency by offering a good rate of return to those who hold deposits in that currency. Using foreign currency reserves to buy its own currency and raising interest rates are the two main ways in which a government can 'defend' or 'prop up' a weakening currency. The British government used both measures in 1992 to defend the pound against George Soros' speculation. In the event, it was unsuccessful and was forced to accept the consequent fall of sterling's value.

Rising global demand for the goods or commodities exported by a country strengthens its currency, and vice versa. This is because the countries that are importing those goods and commodities need to purchase the currency in order to buy them, which increases demand for it. Rapidly falling commodity prices (reflecting falling demand) are a feature of the current crisis, and are putting the currencies of commodity exporters under enormous pressure.

In the long term, the strength of a currency depends on how attractive its host country (or zone) is to investors. Countries like the US with political stability and favourable tax regimes attract high levels of foreign investment, keeping demand for the dollar high.

In general terms, a strong currency favours importers, while a weak currency favours exporters by making their exports more affordable to foreign purchasers. However, a very weak currency is extremely dangerous for countries that need to import food or other crucial items, as it reduces their ability to pay for these imports.

'Well, you know, I was
a human being before I
became a businessman.'
George Soros

Will the eurozone fare better than the UK?

In early November 2008 the European Commission forecast a worse economic performance over the next two years in the UK than in any other European economies apart from Latvia and Estonia. It predicted a 1% fall in UK GDP in 2009, against 0.1% growth for the eurozone as a whole.

If these forecasts prove accurate, the UK's poor performance will have little to do with any benefits the euro has to offer. Instead, it will reflect the size of the UK's deflating housing bubble and the exposure of its financial sector to toxic debt. Indeed, the outlook for the UK would probably be even worse as part of the eurozone, as (unlike the eurozone countries) it retains national control over its own interest rates, one of the major instruments by which recession can be tackled.

The outlook within the eurozone is complicated. Some countries will fare better than others, with recession inflicting most pain on those economies that are generally weakest. Thus Germany is likely to do well, given its low level of household debt and the resilience of its exports. Italian exporters, on the other hand, have been losing ground to Asian manufacturers of textiles and clothing for some years. This loss of competitiveness, coupled with widespread corruption and an inflexible labour market, does not augur well. Spain and Ireland, with their property busts and high consumer debt, could also have a hard time.

What role has the euro played?

This is the first major crisis in the euro's short history, and along with the other world currencies it has fallen sharply relative to the dollar.

The chink in the euro's armoury is arguably the performance of the European Central Bank (ECB). There is widespread suspicion that European banks have deposited large amounts of toxic assets with the ECB. But the ECB is providing scant information about the extent of these assets, and how it is accounting for them. This could prove a ticking bomb not just for the ECB, but also for the currency it oversees.

A potential problem will come from the disparate effects of the crisis on the fifteen constituent member countries of the eurozone. There is a risk that this will create fatal tensions, with each country going its own way to take back full control over monetary policy. For instance, eurozone countries are committed to keeping annual government borrowing lower than 3% of GDP, but weaker economies such as Italy will need to borrow more than stronger ones like Germany and will find it hard to remain within these limits.

One thing is certain: Britain will not be joining the euro in the near future, if ever.

How has Eastern Europe been affected?

The crisis has exposed severe weaknesses in several Central and Eastern European economies that until recently were regarded as success stories. High levels of public and private foreign debt, undisciplined public spending and weak governments have all played their part. The worst affected, Hungary and the Ukraine, have had to ask the IMF and the European Central Bank for multi-billion-dollar bailouts, necessary to prevent international lenders from withdrawing their loans and bankrupting the countries.

Ukraine's over-reliance on steel exports is at the root of its vulnerability. A collapse in international steel prices, precipitated by falling Chinese demand and a shortage of global credit, caused a collapse in the currency and the resulting need for bailout cash.

Ukraine's economic woes have geopolitical as well as economic ramifications, making it vulnerable to blackmail from its richer neighbour Russia, which makes no secret of its wish to draw Ukraine further within its sphere of influence. Domestic politics are split into two hostile factions, embodied in a strongly pro-Russian President and a Prime Minister who favours closer integration with western economies and eventual membership of the EU.

Ukraine has been forced to postpone a general election to deal with the crisis.

What happened in Iceland?

Iceland's economy had been growing fast during the first decade of the 21st century. Unemployment was low and income per head was above the European Union average. Large investments in energy and aluminium smelting had been financed by foreign investors, and exports seemed assured for years to come.

But at the same time the financial system grew out of all proportion to the size of the domestic economy. By the end of 2007, Iceland's three largest banks had amassed assets abroad of $180 billion, almost five times the size of Iceland's external balance of trade, which is founded on fishing and farming. More importantly, these assets were bought with money borrowed not from depositors, but in the wholesale money markets. The household sector in Iceland was also heavily indebted, even more so than in Britain and the USA.

Once Lehman Brothers went bankrupt in September 2008 and the world's wholesale money markets froze up, the writing was on the wall for Iceland. The government tried to bail out one bank, but with a collapsing currency and a worsening credit position, it was forced to allow two other large banks to default. Given the limited resources of the Icelandic government, the small size of the economy and the disproportionately large scale of the banks' operations, the government has had to resort to seeking loans from Russia and the IMF, which has recently made Iceland a $2.1 billion loan.

Could the same thing happen elsewhere, for instance in Ireland?

The names are similar, but the issues are different. Ireland is suffering from an old-fashioned property bust, but its financial sector does not have Iceland's huge exposure to the global money markets.

Ireland's explosion in property prices began with membership of the eurozone in 1999. With the help of EU grants, the sector was dramatically expanded. When the flow of credit dried up in late 2007, Irish banks were exposed to the property sector to the tune of €105 billion.

The falling property market caused alarm among Irish banks about the sector's ability to service its loans. This was judged by the Irish central bank to threaten the solvency of some institutions. The Irish government therefore issued a unilateral guarantee to all savers that their entire deposits with local banks would be safe. The extent of the guarantee was greater than that available in the UK or indeed in the rest of Europe, and some foreign savers moved their money to Irish banks to take advantage if it.

While Irish depositors rejoiced, the country attracted opprobrium from elsewhere in the EU for its unilateral action, potentially in breach of EU rules. In the wake of the property crisis, Ireland went into recession with GDP contracting a full percentage point over a single quarter.

How is the crisis affecting China?

The consensus until a few months ago was that China would be largely immune to the financial crisis, but it now looks vulnerable to a downturn. Economic growth has shrunk rapidly from 12% annually to 9%. This has been accompanied by a collapse in its property market and rising inflation.

The gathering recession has taken its toll on global demand for Chinese goods, causing the closure of several factories. As in the west, Chinese banks are suffering the after-effects of excessive lending to the private sector, and have been hit by high levels of default. The drying-up of credit has caused the collapse of the formerly buoyant real estate markets in many Chinese cities.

But China is better off than other emerging economies, such as Brazil or South Africa. Unlike these countries, it is not dependent for its wealth on commodities, the prices of which have fallen precipitously as the world goes into recession. In fact, China will benefit from falling commodity prices, since it needs to import huge quantities of steel and other raw materials to feed its manufacturing sector.

Moreover, China has vast foreign exchange reserves, totalling almost $2 trillion. Along with its fiscal position, among the healthiest of any large economy, this should help China to withstand the next few months or years better than most.

How is India being affected?

India's GDP has grown 8% annually over the last three years, making it the world's fastest growing economy after China. But now India is waking up to the fact that globalisation can bring problems as well as prosperity.

In the first nine months of 2008, foreign investors hit by credit shortages at home withdrew $11 billion of investment from India. This has resulted in very sharp drops in prices on local stock exchanges. The Indian currency, the rupee, has also fallen to its lowest level to the dollar for six years. The Indian central bank is reported to have spent $8 billion to prop up the rupee, whose fall risks triggering local inflation by increasing the cost of imported goods.

Although Indian banks have avoided excessive exposure to the sub-prime meltdown in the US, its banks are buckling under the strain of disinvestment and global market pressures. The Indian government has been forced to inject $21 billion into the local banking system, and has also had to bail out the mutual fund sector, both of which have struggled as investors seek to cash in their investments.

Like China, India will benefit from falling commodity prices and the collapse in the rupee will help its exports. But with a relatively small cushion of foreign exchange reserves and a comparatively weak external trade position, it is vulnerable to further shocks.

How is Russia faring?

Not well. The Moscow stock exchange plummeted as the crisis took hold. On several occasions disorderly trading forced the authorities to close the floor.

In recent years, Russia's corporate sector has built up high levels of debt, mainly to foreign lenders. Russian companies will have to repay or refinance an estimated $40 billion of debt by the end of 2008, and $150 billion by the end of 2009. As ready sources of credit on the international money markets have run dry, the government is having to come to the rescue. It has already set aside $50 billion for this, with state loans to be secured against company shares. If these loans are not repaid on time, companies that were only recently privatised (after the fall of communism) will return to state ownership.

The banking sector, inadequately policed and riddled with corruption, has also suffered, and has so far required a $36 billion bailout from the government.

Russia (and its currency, the rouble) will suffer from falls in oil, gas and other commodity prices, since these make up most of its exports. The country's large foreign exchange reserves – estimated at more than $600 billion before the start of the crisis – give the government some room for maneoeuvre. However, these reserves began to shrink very rapidly in late 2008, and it remains to be seen whether they will be sufficient to shield the currency and the wider economy from collapse.

What is happening in Japan?

When today's crisis struck, Japan was still recovering from the bursting of a domestic property bubble in the early 1990s. The country's experience then has many parallels with what is happening now in the west. Excessive lending resulted in the collapse of property and share prices, and several banks had to be recapitalised.

Japan is once again in economic difficulties, partly as a result of a huge rise in the yen on the global currency exchanges. The origins of this can be traced to the very low Japanese interest rates in the early 90s, which fell as low as 0% for a time. This gave rise to what is known as the 'carry trade': investors borrowing the yen at very cheap rates in order to convert into higher-yielding alternatives.

However, the fall of these other currencies against the yen has now prompted speculators to reverse their positions and buy back yen in order to avoid suffering big losses on the exchange rate. The resulting dramatic appreciation of the currency is very painful for Japan's exporters, making them uncompetitive in the global marketplace. The usual central bank response would be to cut interest rates, but Japan's rates are so low that there is little scope for this.

The huge sums the Japanese banks have lent in yen also leave them exposed to the risk of mass defaults if borrowers have used the money to buy toxic assets, for example in the US mortgage markets, and therefore find themselves unable to repay.

Has the crisis affected Africa and the world's poorest countries?

The world's poorest countries are exposed to the economic crisis on two main fronts: through reductions in aid, and through falls in commodity prices.

There is good reason to fear that western governments will cut back on aid as they grapple with domestic demands on their finances. Voters in the developed world will expect their governments to attend to pressing domestic problems rather than spend money and time extending support to other countries.

Many of the world's poorest countries rely heavily on exports of raw materials, and so will be badly affected by collapsing commodity prices. Lower demand for their exports will weaken currencies in these commodity-driven economies. The results could be disastrous, especially in countries that do not grow enough food to support their populations. A weak currency could mean that they are unable to afford to import sufficient food from other countries, and force them to turn to the international community for financial aid.

Will the crisis have any impact on international efforts to combat global warming?

This is a political as much as an economic issue. Politicians will come under pressure to allocate resources to areas of the economy hit by the financial crisis in order to relieve their population's immediate woes. This may mean funds and attention are diverted away from the expensive development of alternative, greener energy sources.

In the EU, there are signs that commitments to fighting climate change are weakening in the face of economic pressures. Countries are worried that imposing extra costs on carbon emissions will cause some traditional, high carbon industries such as steel to move elsewhere, resulting in job losses and further economic stress. At an EU summit in October 2008, the Italian Prime Minister, Silvio Berlusconi, proposed that meeting carbon-cutting targets should wait until the financial crisis is over.

There are two weak shafts of light in this very cloudy sky. First, governments may decide to bring forward the construction of large renewable energy projects as part of job-creating initiatives. Second, the amount of polluting carbon emissions is likely to fall a little as economic activity contracts during the recession.

Will the global balance of economic power change?

The crisis is unlikely to affect long-term global trends. The credit crunch and recession have exposed weaknesses in the most dynamic new economies such as China, as well as in the more established capitalist economies of the west.

Among the largest emerging economies, it is likely that Brazil and Russia will fare worse than China and India. This is because they are more dependent on commodity exports and so will be worse hit by falls in oil, food and other prices.

However, China's fledgeling market economy has never been tested by crisis, and it remains to be seen how effectively it will weather the storm. Economic hardship may expose weaknesses in civil society, and bring latent tensions between different social and economic groups to the surface. Heavy job losses in the manufacturing sector will affect many who have recently moved from villages to the city and could create a disaffected, rootless, politically and socially disruptive proletariat.

It seems probable that the US will suffer some loss of international credibility, since the crisis is widely perceived to have its origins in the unrestrained practices of its financial institutions. One result of this may be increased pressure from wealthy emerging economies for an equal place at the negotiating table of such multilateral institutions as the IMF.

Is this the end of globalisation, and the start of a new protectionist era?

It is an exaggeration to say that globalisation has come to an end. But it is equally reasonable to speculate that we will see an upsurge in economic nationalism and a retreat into protectionism in various forms. Governments will come under pressure to fight fires at home. Electorates will expect their domestic interests to take precedence over those of international groupings, such as the World Trade Organisation or the European Union.

The economic events of the 1930s perhaps provide a salutary analogy. Prior to this crisis, the world's economy, a less complex and more manageable affair with fewer important players than today, was fairly well integrated. Governments worked in concert and companies across the world moved in step. The crisis between 1929 and 1933 broke up economic alliances. Ultimately, the global polity fell apart to disastrous effect. After the Second World War, countries came together again to rebuild the economic system. The structures they created – such as the IMF and the World Bank – ushered in a period of globalisation. They are now facing their most stringent test.

5

And another thing...

Did anyone foresee the crisis?

Many observers without axes to grind foresaw a crisis of some kind, though perhaps not in the form it eventually took. Martin Wolf of the *Financial Times* regularly expressed his belief that a dangerous bubble was inflating in western property markets, and that the imbalances in the world economy – with Asia financing a spending spree in the west – would eventually have to be painfully corrected.

There were also worries about the massive size of the global derivatives market. These financial instruments represent a bet on the behaviour of another asset. At the time of the Iraq war, Warren Buffett dubbed derivatives 'Financial Weapons of Mass Destruction'. The Bank for International Settlements, an organisation based in Basel which produces rules for banks, issued very stern warnings about the situation from 2005 onwards. George Soros, another leading American investor, warned that derivatives carried very significant risks as long ago as the turn of the decade.

These warnings were disregarded by policy makers who, like the Lotus Eaters in Homer's *Odyssey*, were lulled into a state of insouciant well-being by a climate of low inflation, low interest rates and stable growth. They failed to see the Scylla of recession and the Charybdis of credit contraction until it was too late to avert a crash.

Should any blame be laid at the door of the British government?

Prime Minister Gordon Brown's record deserves some scrutiny because of the policies he implemented while Chancellor of the Exchequer.

Brown was responsible for setting up and overseeing the Financial Services Authority (FSA) which instigated a 'light touch' regulatory regime. With the benefit of hindsight, the FSA should have scrutinised banks' balance sheets more carefully, and flagged up their excessive reliance on the short-term wholesale money markets to fund long-term mortgage lending. It should also have taken a more sceptical view of the widespread and massive use of derivatives as a means of transferring risk.

During his tenure as Chancellor, Brown promulgated the belief that the economy could motor ever upwards. The Bank of England Monetary Policy Committee, set up when he first came to power, was independent, but may have felt under pressure to cut interest rates whenever there seemed any danger of an economic slowdown. This enabled investors in housing to bid up prices to the point where they were unsustainable.

Brown was not alone. It is easy to believe that there isn't a cloud in the sky when inflation is low and the economy is growing. Especially given the UK's record of unbroken economic growth over the last 16 years.

How similar was the Great Crash of 1929?

Like today's, the crash of 1929 came after a period of very rapid credit expansion that culminated in disastrous levels of non-payment and a subsequent contraction of credit. To that extent, it is similar. However, there are also significant differences.

The 1929 crash began in the stock market, before spreading to the banks. Banks were hit because they had been lending against the security of stock (that is, using stocks and shares as collateral). As stock prices fell, the banks required the customers to whom they had made loans to put up more and more collateral. Large numbers were forced to default, and a systemic banking crisis followed, as panicked depositors withdrew their savings *en masse*.

Today's crisis began in the financial sector, specifically in the US sub-prime mortgage market, rather than in the stock market. The resulting 'credit crunch', as banks rebuild capital to make good their losses, has ensured its spread to the real economy, which is dependent on the availability of credit for normal functioning.

Unlike in 1929, people aren't rushing to draw their money from bank accounts and stash it under their mattresses. But vast sums of money are being withdrawn from the private sector and put into safer government bills. The result, now as then, is a vicious circle of financial contraction.

Have the markets lost credibility?

The violence of recent swings in the financial markets may have weakened people's faith, at least in the short term, in the market's ability to set prices and allocate capital rationally. Markets are only as rational as the investors who drive them. Irrational forces such as greed, 'wishful thinking' and fear are showing few signs of disappearing from the human psyche.

However, it is worth remembering that the cycle of 'boom and bust' in market economies is nothing new. It is very unlikely that recent events will give rise to a radically different, non-market-based system.

'We will never return to
the old boom and bust.'

Gordon Brown

Should technology take any of the blame?

Technology accounts for the breakneck speed at which the crisis has travelled. In part, this is because news and opinion have been disseminated so quickly. One medium for this has been the internet, where bloggers have acted as conduits for rumours, sometimes with little or no foundation, to investors hungry for every last tidbit of information.

Technology has also played a role in the failure to appreciate the risks inherent in the asset-backed securities market. Sophisticated computer programs were designed to base their analysis on data that only went back as far as the mid-nineties, with the result that their analysis did not sufficiently take into account the possibility of a fall in house prices. However, the fault here lies as much with the programmer as with the programmed.

The evolution in the derivatives and other financial markets of daunting levels of complexity, beyond the capacity of human brains to understand easily, has also been aided by computers.

'The government is like a handicapped turtle trying to crawl around and keep up with the rabbit, which is technology.'
James Breithaupt

What happened to the huge profits banks used to make?

The profits that once attracted so much opprobrium (and envy) have been dispersed in three directions.

Some have been channeled wisely towards building up reserves of capital. In recent months banks have had to draw heavily on these reserves to absorb losses made on unwise investments. However, most have found that their reserves have been insufficient and have had to raise new capital from the government or other sources.

Some profits have been paid out to shareholders in the form of the (very generous) dividends common to the sector. Pension funds, as major shareholders in UK banks, have been among the largest recipients.

And some profits – in the UK, an estimated £31 billion over the past four years – have been used to pay bonuses to bankers.

As a significant shareholder in many UK banks, the government has now placed constraints on what banks can do with their profits. For instance, the nationalised banks are not permitted to pay out dividends until they have redeemed the preference shares held by the government. They are also forbidden to award cash bonuses to their employees.

If we had been using Shari'a banking principles would the crisis have happened?

Shari'a banking principles are those applied in Islamic banking, a growing but still minor presence on the international banking scene. At their core is the prohibition of interest (in Arabic, 'riba'). Other religions, including Judaism, have a similar prohibition on usury and rent. The idea is that money should be earned by providing a real service or good: making money merely by handling money is viewed as immoral.

However, Shari'a finance operates in the real world, and few Muslim countries adhere rigidly to this principle. In practice, it translates into a general unease about financial instruments that detach an investment from its intrinsic value. So derivative-style instruments and other complex investment products do not sit easily with Shari'a principles.

Today's crisis has been exacerbated by the growth of a huge derivatives market that the application of Shari'a banking principles would have prevented from developing. Nevertheless, it is unlikely that we will see large numbers of contrite Wall Street or City of London bankers signing up to the Shari'a banking code.

Will there be a transfer of power from financial institutions to government?

One interpretation of recent events is that they have shown power to reside more with governments than with financial institutions, many of which have had to rely on government help to survive.

In the short term, the British government will certainly exercise more influence over financial institutions, given that they are now part-owners of many of them. For instance, they are approving members to the boards of these instiutions, and have attached several conditions to their provision of bailout finance. Such direct methods of control will cease once the banks have succeeded in redeeming the preference shares held by the government, and once the government has chosen to sell its ordinary shares in the banks. It is not known exactly when this will be.

Western governments will also come under pressure to tighten the regulations operating in the financial sector, in order to prevent a recurrence of the excesses that spawned the current crisis. This could be seen as a shift in power away from financial institutions towards governments.

In Russia, there is a real possibility that banks and other companies will again come under state control. The Russian government's loans are secured on company shares; the cost of defaulting will be a return to state ownership.

How much does Barack Obama know about economics?

While America's economic woes were a constant refrain in the final stages of the US election, neither candidate showed any in-depth knowledge of economic theory. However, John McCain dealt his claim to the presidency a fatal blow by admitting that he was not interested in economics. This was at a time when the crunch had yet to reach its zenith, but it came back to haunt him as recession beckoned. On the night of the election, exit polls showed that the economy was the most important issue for seven out of ten voters.

The world will look to President Obama for leadership in combatting the crisis, but his own economic expertise is less important than that of his advisers. Their ability to provide sound analysis and sensible recommendations will influence our economic well-being for years to come.

'This is the final verdict on the failed economic policies of the last eight years.'

Barack Obama

6

Can we stop this happening again?

Can a similar crisis be avoided in the future?

Some people might say that boom and bust is an unwelcome but inevitable characteristic of the free market economy. Financial collapses have occurred throughout history. In Holland in the 17th century, tulip mania reached incredible heights – a single bulb could sell for more than twenty times a worker's annual income – but then the market collapsed, resulting in the ruin of countless investors. There was the disastrous South Seas bubble in the 18th century, the infamous 1929 Wall Street Crash and the bursting of the Dot-Com bubble in 2001, to name a few. So how can we avoid a repeat performance?

Recent events have made us all too aware that the current system by which banks and other financial institutions are regulated is dysfunctional. Many believe that it should become more rigorous and interventionist, with regulators working together to ensure the overall security of the market.

How effective tighter regulation will be, and how long it will stay in place, remains to be seen. Having come so close to ruin, it is likely that the banks will tread carefully, for a while at least. But the global economy is an unruly animal with a short memory. It is not impossible that future prosperity may eventually induce the same risk-taking behaviour on the part of investors, and the same laissez-faire attitude on the part of the regulators, that led to the latest disaster.

Will financial institutions be subject to more regulation in future?

There is a great deal of talk about regulation, and the system is in line for an overhaul. Many of the activities that contributed to the crisis – for example, the over-zealous trading in securities and derivatives – have fallen into disrepute. People are stunned by the extent of the chaos and will be looking for ways to bring the markets under control.

So yes, it is very likely that financial institutions will end up subject to a firmer system of 'rules-based' regulation. Rules-based regulation, where actions and compliance are specified, will lead to an increase in transparency as institutions make efforts to prove that they have complied with the rules. Regulation is also likely to be much more interventionist than in the past.

In the short term, many governments are now major shareholders of international banking institutions. Doubtless they will take more of an interest in the reports and actions of the regulators now that they (and the taxpayers they represent) hold such a significant stake.

Do regulators need to broaden their organisations?

Yes they do, and it is likely to happen. There are many regulatory bodies in place both nationally and internationally, such as the Financial Services Authority, the Bank of England, the European Central Bank and the US Federal Reserve. All of them bear some responsibility for what has happened, and all of them will be seeking to clarify and strengthen their influence.

One of the problems is that regulation and regulatory bodies have not globalised in line with the banks they oversee. Regulators are often restrained by national boundaries and domestic priorities. Commentators and politicians, including Gordon Brown, have argued for a global architecture for banking regulation that reflects the global reach of the world's largest institutions. This is a worthy but challenging objective: efforts have been made in the past to find a structure which can deal with the diversity of local markets, practices and law, but they have foundered.

However, the scale of the recent crisis has ensured that governments around the world *are* working together, and at the time of writing there is a more unified, international momentum towards tackling the problems of the global economy.

Does everyone agree that more regulation of the financial sector is a good idea?

More regulation means less market freedom. Dyed-in-the-wool market participants will loathe the thought that government and its foot soldiers, the regulators, will be passing more rules and intervening more actively in the markets. They believe that a market controlled by guidelines, restrictions and rules will lose its edge and become less competitive, to the detriment of society as a whole.

So for a long time markets resisted regulation, and the extraordinary prosperity of recent years seemed vindication enough. Now, though, with recent dramatic events exposing flaws in our complex systems, many agencies are working towards a new, improved, broader and stronger regulatory system.

However, some people believe that it is the regulators, rather than regulatory system itself, that have let the market down, and that greater leadership and more highly skilled personnel are needed within the sector.

Are governments encouraging bad bankers by rescuing them?

It is true that if you go around bailing out people who have got into trouble it might encourage them to act carelessly in the future. Such a situation is termed 'moral hazard', where a party is immune from the negative effects of their actions. Knowing that someone else will bail you out almost certainly encourages a heedless, devil-may-care attitude.

The bailout may not have been the ideal way to inculcate prudence in an often inherently risk-taking environment, but if governments hadn't stepped in with some sort of rescue package there was a real possibility that the economy would collapse. While many would like to see bankers hung out to dry, the government's rescue measures have limited the damage and saved many of us from facing severe consequences. It is also worth mentioning that if banks had been allowed to go under, some of the biggest losers would have been large insitutional investors in the banking sector, among them pension funds. Many people on the brink of retirement would have suddenly found themselves in catastrophically straitened circumstances.

Have bankers paid any sort of price?

Well yes, some of them. There have been job-losses, redundancies, suspended bonuses. Those who have hung on to their jobs are working in a more insecure and stressful environment. And over and above the general gloom haunting the banking sector, there is a possibility that disciplinary measures – possibly even criminal charges – are on the cards for some.

For many people this simply is not good enough. However, the truth is that this crisis is just too big to apportion blame. It is everybody's fault, and nobody's. A surfeit of money circulating in America, thanks to booming Far Eastern economies, was channeled through the Federal Reserve to US mortgage giants Fannie Mae and Freddie Mac. The (not unworthy) goal was housing for all, but it led directly to the disastrously contagious sub-prime mortgage bubble.

At the other end of the spectrum, the average consumer, running up excessive debts in the housing market and on the high street, is culpable to a degree. When there is a huge supply of money, markets function like unstoppable machines. Singling out a particular sector of the banking industry would not be fair.

Do credit rating agencies need more regulation?

Credit rating agencies (CRAs) are right at the heart of the failed system. A shake-up looks inevitable.

It is hard to overstate their importance. Famous CRAs like Standard & Poor's, Moody's and Fitch are the examiners who grade an institution or a financial product. The investing community relies on these bodies to tell them whether an institution or product is sound. The rating agency bases its grades on the likelihood that an institution – which can include a government – will default on a loan. It's clear that they did not deliver the necessary warnings at the appropriate time; the system did not work.

Many people claim that the CRAs were insufficiently objective, giving in to pressure from banks to award positive ratings for toxic assets. The basis of this accusation lies in a possible flaw in the system: that the institution being assessed is also the one footing the bill. Whether it is a bank, a government or a central reserve, the fact that the agencies are funded by the institutions they examine means that their impartiality may be compromised.

This structural flaw will have to be dealt with. Thought must also be given to the quality of CRA staff. Banks have the upper hand in the pay stakes and tend to attract the more technically gifted analysts and economists. Governments need to work out how the agencies can stay ahead of the banks.

Should hedge funds be more regulated?

There are many different types of hedge funds with widely varying strategies. They have become associated with high levels of risk-taking, but this is not true of all hedge funds. Indeed, their original function was to reduce risk by 'hedging' other financial positions. However, many modern funds do not actually hedge their investments, and use short-selling, aggressive leveraging and other methods to increase rather than reduce risk, with the aim of increasing returns.

Hedge funds are subject to less regulation than other financial institutions. Their assets, liabilities and trading activities are not publicly disclosed, and they operate under less rigorous capital requirements, freeing them to borrow more. Historically, this can be explained by the fact that they are only open to a small number of sophisticated private investors, assumed to be aware of the risks entailed. However, the recent massive growth of hedge funds means that their actions can cause shockwaves in the wider financial system. Many believe it is now time to tighten their regulation.

The typical hedge fund has a company in an offshore location with a relaxed regulatory regime. This is where the money is kept. A second company administrates the fund and is based in a financial centre with legal and accounting skills, perhaps Dublin. A third company is based in a city such as London with strong investment skills. Such geographical fragmentation makes regulation difficult.

Will short-selling be banned for good?

In short-selling, speculators profit from a fall on the stock market, rather than a rise. The speculator 'borrows' or 'rents' the product to be sold, perhaps from a bank or a pension fund, before selling it on to a third party (who may not know that he is participating in the short-selling process). If all goes according to plan, the value of the shares will then fall on the stock market, at which point the speculator buys identical shares and returns them to the lender. He profits from selling borrowed shares high, buying replacement shares low and pocketing the difference. Of course if the speculator gambles incorrectly and prices rise, he will make a loss.

Shorting has come under attack for contributing to the volatility of the stock markets. Some believe that large investors were working together to force prices down before buying back their stock. In October 2008, short-selling was probably taking place in the stock of HBOS, while Richard Fuld, CEO of Lehman Brothers in the US, blames short-selling for the unstoppable downward trajectory of his company's shares.

In the US, short-selling was temporarily banned in an attempt to restore equilibrium, but since the markets fell a further 23% while the ban was in effect, it is debatable whether it achieved anything. Some experts have criticised the ban, labelling it a knee-jerk reaction.

Should commercial banks and investment banks be separated?

Possibly, but any suggestion that we can break up the leviathans of the banking world is pie in the sky. Indeed, regulators have found themselves encouraging conglomeration in order to stave off some of the worst effects of the credit crisis. Take, for example, the government-backed merger of Lloyds-TSB and failing bank HBOS, which sees two of the five biggest UK banks come together.

The problem lies in the way high street banks have invested their depositors' funds. Banks that take deposits from the public have been involved in risky trading more properly associated with investment banking. Some commentators have likened conventional banking activity (payments and deposits) to a utility, and investment banks to a casino. When the utility plays with people's deposits in the casino, the risks are spread wide across society. Martin Wolf, a respected *Financial Times* commentator, put it this way: 'We have allowed banks to provide both an essential utility function on which the entire economic system depends, and at the same time gamble freely and at will with next to no capital behind them, essentially at the taxpayers' expense. That is not tolerable.'

This investment approach might be a good deal safer if proper regulatory precautions were in place, but the whole business has become so fiendishly complex that many regulators failed to keep abreast of the risks banks were running. In fact, some of the banks were themselves unaware of the full scale of the risk, much of it emanating from the disastrous sub-prime mortgage market in the US. The loans from this sector were bundled together and packaged up before being traded and re-traded until they were almost unrecognisable.

There may be a call to restore the American-led Glass-Steagall Act of 1933 which separated out commercial and investment banking activities during the Great Depression. The repeal of this law in 1999, at a time of amnesia-inducing prosperity, was probably unwise, but it is unlikely that bankers and brokers can ever be fully separated. It is crucial for long-term social and economic health that the integrity of savers' deposits should be protected. Tougher regulation may be the way forward.

'If you owe your bank a hundred pounds, you have a problem. But if you owe a million, it has.'

J. M. Keynes

What should I do with my money – spend or save?

Though the future is not ours to see, it is likely that most long-term investments will recoup their losses and build on their assets in time. If you are looking to the future, or to future generations, and do not need your money right now, then it probably makes sense to invest it. The stock markets will recover eventually, though it may take years or even – in the worst case scenario – decades. And there are also the more stolid options like government bonds with lower rates of interest but almost guaranteed returns.

However this is not to say that you should neglect your investments. Everyone should keep an eye on their finances and review them regularly (with the help of an independent expert if possible).

In the meantime we are going to go through some form of recession. Although spending one's way out of a recession has in recent times once again become a popular notion, it makes sense to act with caution and curb current spending, at least until the repercussions of today's crisis become clearer.

Can a major global recession be avoided?

We have moved beyond the point where a recession in the developed world can be avoided. The issue is how deep the recession will be and how long it will last.

The solution most favoured by governments in developed countries is to boost state spending on infrastructure in order to maintain levels of employment and put spending power into as many pockets as possible. The government may also cut taxes in the short term in order to encourage consumers out onto the streets. Small businesses who have been squeezed by a lack of credit will be some of the greatest beneficiaries here. The United States government may have set a precedent that other countries will follow when it made an ex gratia payment to all citizens to return some taxes to their pockets.

Meanwhile there is little to do but tighten our belts and wait to see what happens. The economy has to go through a dour period of correction, and at the time of writing the jury is still out on just how bad things are going to get. Some are forecasting a brief recession, a short interruption in the onward march of global prosperity. Others more gloomily interpret the current situation as the prelude to something altogether more serious. Only time will tell.

GLOSSARY

ASSET-BACKED SECURITIES

Securities with a supposedly predictable income stream based on 'bundles' of different assets, such as home loans, car loans and credit card loans.

BONDS, GILTS

A form of IOU: an agreement under which a sum is repaid to an investor with interest after a specified period of time. Gilts are bonds issued by the government.

DERIVATIVE

A security whose value depends on (i.e. is 'derived' from) the value of another underlying security. Can be thought of as a bet on the future value of the underlying security.

FINANCIAL INSTRUMENT

A general term referring to the legal obligation of one party to transfer something of value (usually money) to another party at some future date, under certain conditions.

GROSS DOMESTIC PRODUCT (GDP)

The standard measure of the size of a national economy. It is the total value of goods and services produced in one year within a country's borders.

HEDGE FUND

A fund, often aggressively managed, that uses sophisticated investment strategies such as leverage, long, short and derivative positions in both domestic and international markets with the goal of generating high returns.

INFLATION

The increase of prices over time.

LIBOR, LONDON INTERBANK OFFERED RATE

The rate of interest at which banks lend money to each other.

MONEY MARKETS, CAPITAL MARKETS

The financial markets in which funds are borrowed or loaned for short periods (less than one year). They are generally open only to banks and other financial institutions.

NEGATIVE EQUITY

When the current market value of a property is less than the amount owed on the mortgage.

PREFERENCE SHARES

Shares in a company with a fixed dividend that takes preference over dividends to common shareholders. They do not usually have voting rights.

RECESSION

A decrease in economic activity for two consecutive quarters. A severe recession is known as a depression.

SECURITIES

Any type of transferable certificate of ownership, including equity (shares) and debt.

SECURITISATION

The pooling together of similar loans (e.g. home mortgages) so that they can be made available to prospective investors, usually in the form of bonds.

SHORT-SELLING

The practice of selling a financial instrument that the seller does not own at the time of the sale. Short-selling is done with the intention of later purchasing the financial instrument at a lower price.

SUB-PRIME MORTGAGE

A loan to a property owner with a heightened perceived risk of non-payment, owing to a history of loan delinquency or default, a recorded bankruptcy or limited debt experience.

Index

ACKNOWLEDGEMENTS

The authors would like to acknowledge the guidance and help of Stephen Lewis, the chief economist at Monument Securities, and Stephen Powell, an independent economist and consultant. Peter Hahn of Cass Business School, George Magnus, senior adviser to UBS Investment Bank and Martin Wolf of the *Financial Times* also gave valuable advice. The authors take full responsibility for all opinions expressed.

Some material has been sourced from *The Bank of England Financial Stability Report* and *The National Institute of Economic and Social Research Review.*

Help was also received from Brian Zlotnick and Julius Kochan. Caroline Pym and Miriam Kochan assisted in diverse but invaluable ways. The Pym and Kochan families have shown their customary forbearance and that has been appreciated.

Ben Yarde-Buller and David Reynolds of Old Street Publishing conceived of this project and the authors are grateful to them.